W9-ARI-266

BLACKBIRD

BY DAVID HARROWER

★

★

DRAMATISTS
PLAY SERVICE
INC.

BLACKBIRD
Copyright © 2007, David Harrower

All Rights Reserved

CAUTION: Professionals and amateurs are hereby warned that performance of BLACKBIRD is subject to payment of a royalty. It is fully protected under the copyright laws of the United States of America, and of all countries covered by the International Copyright Union (including the Dominion of Canada and the rest of the British Commonwealth), and of all countries covered by the Pan-American Copyright Convention, the Universal Copyright Convention, the Berne Convention, and of all countries with which the United States has reciprocal copyright relations. All rights, including without limitation professional/amateur stage rights, motion picture, recitation, lecturing, public reading, radio broadcasting, television, video or sound recording, all other forms of mechanical, electronic and digital reproduction, transmission and distribution, such as CD, DVD, the Internet, private and file-sharing networks, information storage and retrieval systems, photocopying, and the rights of translation into foreign languages are strictly reserved. Particular emphasis is placed upon the matter of readings, permission for which must be secured from the Author's agent in writing.

The English language stock and amateur stage performance rights in the United States, its territories, possessions and Canada for BLACKBIRD are controlled exclusively by DRAMATISTS PLAY SERVICE, INC., 440 Park Avenue South, New York, NY 10016. No professional or nonprofessional performance of the Play may be given without obtaining in advance the written permission of DRAMATISTS PLAY SERVICE, INC., and paying the requisite fee.

Inquiries concerning all other rights should be addressed to Casarotto Ramsay & Associates, Ltd., Waverley House, 7-12 Noel Street, London W1F 8GQ, England. Attn: Mel Kenyon.

SPECIAL NOTE

Anyone receiving permission to produce BLACKBIRD is required to give credit to the Author as sole and exclusive Author of the Play on the title page of all programs distributed in connection with performances of the Play and in all instances in which the title of the Play appears for purposes of advertising, publicizing or otherwise exploiting the Play and/or a production thereof. The name of the Author must appear on a separate line, in which no other name appears, immediately beneath the title and in size of type equal to 50% of the size of the largest, most prominent letter used for the title of the Play. No person, firm or entity may receive credit larger or more prominent than that accorded the Author. The following acknowledgments must appear on the title page in all programs distributed in connection with performances of the Play:

BLACKBIRD was first commissioned and presented
by the Edinburgh International Festival at the King's Theatre, Edinburgh,
in August 2005 and was subsequently presented at the Albery Theatre
in the West End by Michael Edwards and Carole Winter for MJE Productions,
opening on February 13, 2006.

BLACKBIRD was originally produced in the United States
by the Manhattan Theatre Club,
Lynne Meadow, Artistic Director; Barry Grove, Executive Producer,
on March 15, 2007.

For Selma

BLACKBIRD was originally produced in New York City by the Manhattan Theatre Club (Lynne Meadow, Artistic Director; Barry Grove, Executive Producer), opening on March 15, 2007. It was directed by Joe Mantello; the set design was by Scott Pask; the costume design was by Laura Bauer; the lighting design was by Paul Gallo; the sound design was by Darron L. West; the fight director was J. David Brimmer; the production stage manager was Jill Cordle; the stage manager was Neil Krasnow; and the production manager was Ryan McMahon. The cast was as follows:

RAY .... Jeff Daniels
UNA .... Alison Pill

CHARACTERS

UNA

RAY

BLACKBIRD

Una, twenties. Coat, dress, gloves; carries a bag. Ray, mid-fifties. Trousers, shirt, tie. A cell phone clipped to his belt. In a room in which there's a low table, several chairs, several lockers. The door is closed. A swing-top garbage can, full of trash. On the floor, around the chairs, more abandoned trash, food packaging mostly with bits of food still visible. An oblong frosted window through which passing figures can occasionally be seen.

UNA.
   Shock.
RAY.
   Of course.
   Yes.
   Now.
(Pause.)
UNA.
   And
RAY.
   Wait.
(Pause. He goes to the closed door, opens it a small way.)
UNA.
   You were busy.
RAY.
   Yes.
UNA.
   They
RAY.
   I still am busy.
   I was with one of the
   our managers.
   We're in the middle of something.

They
So I might
I could get called away.
I'll be sent for.
I'm still needed.
UNA.
Don't people have homes?
RAY.
Homes?
UNA.
Outside.
RAY.
I don't
UNA.
To go to.
Homes to go to.
They're still working.
It's late.
RAY.
We're finishing soon.
They'll be going soon.
An order came in delayed and
of course
but we have to process it no matter how late.
And late is
The time's not a consideration.
We have to process the order and then dispatch it.
It's a very quick turnaround.
UNA.
Do they go home when you tell them?
RAY.
No.
But I, I make sure all is
when the work's done.
I have to make sure.
UNA.
But so what do you actually make here?
RAY.
It's
Dentistry.

UNA.
    Because
RAY.
    Sometimes pharmaceutical.
UNA.
    The name on the front.
    You can't tell.
    Like one of those low buildings you pass
    I passed
    on the expressway, on the way here.
    Low buildings, always one story, and you, you
    cars parked outside
    no clue what's happening *in*side.
    Only a digital clock thing on the outside telling what the tem-
perature is.
    This is like that.
(Ray's begun to pick up some of the trash.)
    This is where you eat?
RAY.
    No.
    Not in here.
    Not me.
    The staff do.
UNA.
    They shouldn't leave it like this.
    The floor.
(He takes the trash to the garbage can.)
    It's too full.
(He crams it into the garbage can.)
    Where do you eat?
RAY.
    Are you on your own?
UNA.
    Yes.
    You mean alone?
RAY.
    Yes.
    By yourself.
UNA.
    Yes.

9

RAY.

Can you tell me why you're here?

What've you come here for?

UNA.

Do they get breaks?

Cigarette breaks?

Will any of them

RAY.

No.

Too late now.

UNA.

We won't be interrupted?

I don't want people walking in here.

RAY.

What is there to interrupt?

What do you want?

I don't have much time.

UNA.

I saw

RAY.

And to be honest I

UNA.

What?

RAY.

I

I don't *have* to be in here with you.

You know that, don't you?

You're aware of that?

I don't have to stay here.

Do I?

UNA.

No.

You're right.

RAY.

I don't have to listen.

I don't have to say anything.

So

but a few minutes

a couple of minutes and then you'll have to go and

because I'll be needed back.

(He steps on some discarded food in a wrapper, not noticing it.)
UNA.

> Watch.
> Someone's just left it there.
> You should say something about that.

(He picks it up.)
RAY.

> They've been told.
> They're constantly being told.

(He takes the wrapper to the garbage can, pushes it in. A knock at the door. He walks to the door, opens it a small way to see who's there. He steps out, closes it behind him. Una looks around the room, then sits. Ray reenters. He closes the door but not fully; the same width as before.)

> Why don't we go outside?

UNA.

> Where?

RAY.

> Out of here.
> Outside.

UNA.

> No.

RAY.

> The parking lot or the

UNA.

> I'm fine here.

RAY.

> It's

UNA.

> You pushed me in here.

RAY.

> I didn't push

UNA.

> Out of sight.

RAY.

> I didn't push you.
> I brought you in here.

UNA.

> And they'll wonder who I am.

RAY.

> They all saw you.

So yes.

I'm sure they will.

They

UNA.

You kept me waiting, Peter.

I was standing there for

RAY.

What do you want?

Will you

UNA.

Can I close the door?

RAY.

No.

UNA.

Can *you* close the door?

RAY.

The door stays open.

UNA.

Why?

I

RAY.

I don't want it closed.

UNA.

There's a draft.

RAY.

We're going outside in a minute.

UNA.

I'm here now.

You brought me

RAY.

I think this is better outside.

We can

UNA.

Close the door.

(He doesn't move.)

There's a cold draft coming in.

I don't like it.

It's

I'll close it then.

(Pause. She gets up, looks at him, goes to the door. He takes a step

towards her, stops. She pushes the door shut, suddenly, loudly).
> The door's closed.
(She looks at some trash near the door.)
> The people who just
> they expect other people to clean up after them.
> I asked a man
> he dropped an empty can
> beer can
> and a cigarette pack
> on the sidewalk.
> Dropped them.
> Didn't think about it, just let them fall.
> I told him to pick them up.
> He laughed.
> He thought I was joking.
> He was

RAY.
> Will you
(He blinks, rubs at his eyes.)
UNA.
> With a woman.
> Bitch, she called me.
> Defended him.
> He laughed all

RAY.
> How did you find me?
UNA.
> In a
> It was a photo.
> In a magazine.

RAY.
> Where?
> What
UNA.
> Some
RAY.
> Magazine?
UNA.
> Trade magazine.
> Promotional.

A glossy magazine thing, a
in a waiting room.
A doctor's waiting room.
You know the thing I'm talking about?

RAY.

Yes.

UNA.

There was a photo on the back of it.
You and a
with a group of people.
A team.
They called you a team.
You won an award.
Some
Excellence or
performance.

RAY.

So
What?
You saw a photograph?
You saw this photo

UNA.

You have friends?

RAY.

And it
You

UNA.

Friends?

RAY.

Yes.
Of course I have friends, what

UNA.

New friends
or the same old friends?

(Pause.)

Your eyes are red.
They look like they're stinging.

(He laughs briefly to himself, rubbing his eyes again.)

RAY.

What did you feel?

UNA.

Don't rub them.

RAY.

A photo.

So you drove here?

UNA.

Yes.

You want to see it?

RAY.

No I don't want to see it.

UNA.

But you know the photo I'm

RAY.

Yes

UNA.

Stop rubbing them.

RAY.

They hurt.

UNA.

Because you're rubbing them.

RAY.

I rub them *because* they hurt.

It's the only way to stop them from hurting.

You drove here?

UNA.

Yes.

RAY.

How many

how long did it take you?

Where

I don't believe

UNA.

Is it me?

Am I making that happen?

Are you allergic to me?

(Pause. He stares at her.)

Are you not going to talk?

RAY.

We're going to walk outside.

(He moves towards her.)

On your feet.
Will you get up please?
We're going outside.
We're going to walk through the

UNA.

I wrote you letters.

RAY.

Letters?

UNA.

They

RAY.

I never got any letters.

UNA.

They were

RAY.

When?

UNA.

Never sent.

(Pause.)

RAY.

What did they say?
When was this?

UNA.

I wasn't *meant* to send them.
They told me, the people who helped me.
The
who
afterwards
to write you a letter
letters
telling you what I thought of you.
What I felt.
Wanted to say to you.
To not let it
let you have
win.
Authority.
And it was

RAY.

Authority?

What's
UNA.
    I wrote
    hundreds.
    Pull out your eyes.
    I wrote that I wanted to pull out your eyes, wrote
    poke them out, stamp on them.
    To
    All kinds of things.
    I've still got them.
RAY.
    You kept them?
UNA.
    The best ones.
    I still read them sometimes.
    The fury in them.
    You didn't answer.
    New friends?
    Or did your old friends stand by you?
RAY.
    What do you think?
UNA.
    I think
    I think the
RAY.
    Six seven hours to drive here.
    For what?
UNA.
    Because in that photo you're
RAY.
    To make me suffer?
UNA.
    I wouldn't call that
    your eyes
    suffering.
    Rub them more then.
    Harder.
RAY.
    I didn't need to talk to you.
    I could've walked away.

I'm under no obligation
UNA.
So this man
RAY.
What man?
UNA.
That man who dropped the litter, the
it's not the litter
it wasn't the litter
the dirtying.
It was the man, the person doing that.
Because he hasn't been, been
schooled
educated
civilized enough
and I thought,
I just thought you are a beast.
No one has ever cared for you properly and you're too stupid
too stupid to even know that or you wouldn't let other people see
just what a
see what you are.
This
You do not even know you exist.
I asked to speak to Peter.
And Ray appeared.
(Pause.)
RAY.
This was pointless.
Absolutely pointless.
Can you see that?
Can you not see that?
Who told you to do this?
Whoever advised this was
UNA.
No one.
RAY.
I didn't agree to this.
UNA.
No.

RAY.

To get what?

You don't have the right to my my my humiliation.

Where I work.

Where people are.

My colleagues.

Work colleagues.

Walking in, asking for me.

I've nothing to say to you.

I

You're a

some kind of ghost

turning up from nowhere to

Go home.

Please.

Leave me alone.

Go home.

UNA.

You think I still live in the same town?

RAY.

I don't know.

I don't know where you live.

How would I know that?

UNA.

I do.

I still live there.

We

RAY.

Get out of here and

UNA.

never moved.

RAY.

Go back there.

Go back.

UNA.

I do feel like a ghost.

I do.

I feel like a ghost.

Everywhere I go.

I wrote that in my letters too.

You made me into a ghost.
People talked about me as if I wasn't there.
Wouldn't let me speak.

RAY.
Go outside.
Go.
I'm telling you.
Listen to me.
You're
Walk out into the air.
Breathe air.
Get in your car.
Stop being a ghost.
You'll
You will live again.
Because this this this should
should never have happened.
Because are you feeling any better yet?
Is this doing you *good?*

UNA.
Yes.

RAY.
Then that's
That is
I can't say anything to you.
You
You're beyond
How?
How the hell is it good?
Tell me
except
except but you don't know what you want.
You don't know why you're here.
Tell whoever it was sent you

UNA.
Nobody.
I told you.

RAY.
Then I don't care.

(He starts to go.)

UNA.
>Where are you going?

RAY.
>No.

UNA.
>Don't go.

RAY.
>I don't care.
>It's not my responsibility.

UNA.
>I'll follow you.

RAY.
>Do what you want.
>This is
>This is hell.
>Stay away from me.
>You need help.

(He opens the door, goes out.)

UNA.
>Don't leave me in here.
>Ray.

(He reenters, closes the door.)

RAY.
>I have things I have to do.
>I have to check things.
>And
>After.
>When I leave.
>Tonight.
>I have to be places.
>People are relying on me.

UNA.
>What?
>What're you doing?

RAY.
>The thing is
>The
>I don't even know if it *is* you.
>If you're
>her.

UNA.
  I am.
  Of course I am.
RAY.
  I didn't recognize you.
UNA.
  Yes you did.
RAY.
  I didn't.
  I *don't*.
  You.
  No.
UNA.
  Your face went white.
RAY.
  Not
UNA.
  Drained white.
RAY.
  Not not when I first saw you.
  I didn't know who you were
  There's someone here to see you.
  That's all I was told
UNA.
  When I said
RAY.
  Yes
  yes but I know the name.
  I remember the name.
  Jesus the name's
  But you could be a, a friend of hers.
  Your hair's a different color.
  A journalist
  A
UNA.
  I'm not.
RAY.
  Reporter, I don't know.
  I don't know what any of this is about.

UNA.
How many other twelve-year-olds have you had sex with?
(Pause.)
RAY.
None.
UNA.
Do you want to see the birthmark?
You kissed it.
Or what you said on the beach.
Or on the bed in that room in
None?
We change, twelve-year-olds.
We grow up to be older.
So think.
RAY.
None.
UNA.
Just me.
In that room.
I thought it'd be harder to look at you.
To talk.
I almost turned back.
But it's not.
It's easy.
And I would've recognized you anywhere.
With my back to you.
I saw your eyes before I even said my name.
I saw you.
You have someone?
You live with someone?
You don't want to tell me.
I know you're with a woman.
The way I was looked at outside.
The way *you* were looked at when you walked towards me.
A good woman?
Does she
RAY.
I'm not talking about her with
UNA.
Is she expecting you home?

(Pause.)
RAY.

D'you want me to say something?

Is there anything you want me to say now?

UNA.

Does she know about me?

RAY.

I will not say anything about my life.

Who is in my life.

If that's what you wanted to find out and I don't know why you
you would want that

but you're getting nothing.

Do you understand?

Do you understand?

(Pause.)
UNA.

My dad died.

You didn't know?

It didn't reach you?

(He shakes his head.)

Six years ago.

Maybe you weren't here.

Maybe you were somewhere else.

RAY.

I was here.

How?

UNA.

He fell down.

He tripped.

Steps.

And

Deteriorated.

He never got over it.

He

You were a guest in our home.

I was his baby.

He invited you as a guest into his home.

He tried to find you.

RAY.

He knew where I was the first three years, seven months.

UNA.

He wanted to kill you.

Not a second thought.

He said it all the time.

It was

(Louder.)

He would've killed you.

(Ray is startled, unnerved by her loudness and tone. Near tears, Una searches through her bag. Ray watches her, unsettled.)

RAY.

What's in there?

What's in your bag?

What's in it?

UNA.

I need a

RAY.

Give me it

UNA.

No.

Why?

RAY.

What're you doing?

Are you

UNA.

What?

RAY.

Don't.

(He grabs the bag from her.)

UNA.

You're

RAY.

Do you want to kill me?

(Pause. He goes through the bag. He takes out a packet of tissues.)

UNA.

I was going to Kleenex you to death.

(She holds out her hand. He gives her the packet. He takes out a bottle of water.)

And that's acid, not water.

(He takes out the torn page, the photo of him, from the trade magazine. A knock on the door. A voice from behind the door.)

VOICE.
    Peter.
(They look at each other. Ray goes to the door. He opens the door slightly, looks out through the gap.)
RAY.
(To person outside.)
    It's fine.
(He closes the door. He still holds the photo.)
UNA.
    When I saw it I
    the photo.
    It's not clear.
    But I knew it was you.
    I tore it out, took it home, kept
    kept looking at it.
    The name below.
    Peter.
    Peter?
    I couldn't
    I'm so slow sometimes.
    You changed your name.
RAY.
    Yes.
UNA.
    Is that difficult?
RAY.
    No.
    No, it was very easy.
UNA.
    But I mean, decide.
    Decide on a new one.
    Choose a new name.
    Is it hard?
    Do you, do you go through
    how many before you decide?
    Do you make a list?
RAY.
    I chose a name at random.
UNA.
    How?

RAY.

    I opened the phone book

UNA.

    Pin the tail on the donkey.

RAY.

    Kind of.

UNA.

    What's your full name?

    Peter what?

    Peter

    I can ask outside.

RAY.

    Trevelyan.

UNA.

    Peter Trevelyan.

RAY.

    Yes.

(Pause. She gives a quick smile, smothers it.)

UNA.

    Where the hell did that come from?

    Peter *Trevelyan?*

RAY.

    Under T.

    It was necessary.

    It

UNA.

    But

    Jesus.

    Trevelyan

    Did you

    God, no

    That's

    To

    To the manor born.

    The silver spoon.

    It's

    from a phone book at *random?*

    Were you delirious?

    Did

    delusions of of grandeur?

Because

Jesus

The rich sleep

sleep with young girls too.

Underage girls.

Ruin their lives too.

In fact the rich must have as much sex with young girls as the poor.

They must be neck and neck.

But if it does the job

If it

Does it?

Command respect?

And help you

Help you

RAY.

Okay.

UNA.

Forget.

RAY.

Enough.

UNA.

They don't know.

Any of them, outside.

Do they?

And your

the partner?

She

The the lady of the manor.

No one

RAY.

She knows.

UNA.

She knows?

RAY.

Yes.

UNA.

How does she know?

RAY.

I told her.

UNA.

Everything?

RAY.

The facts.

UNA.

My age?

RAY.

Yes.

UNA.

Your sentence?

RAY.

Yes.

UNA.

When?

At the start of the

RAY.

Yes.

We've been together seven years.

UNA.

What did you tell her?

What?

Tell me what you told her?

RAY.

That when I was forty I had

I had an illegal relationship.

I had sex with a minor.

UNA.

And she was fine with that?

RAY.

No.

Of course not.

But I

I told her what my life was like then.

I wasn't in a good way.

I had problems and I didn't

I couldn't handle them.

I gave in.

I broke apart.

UNA.

Did you?

RAY.

I made the biggest
most most stupid mistake of my life.

UNA.

You told her it was a

RAY.

A what?

UNA.

A three-month stupid mistake you made.
That you ran away with me.
That too?

RAY.

And that I
pulled myself up.
I
I got back on track.
I
You laugh.
You don't believe it.
That's fine.
It's fine with me.
I don't need you to.

UNA.

She believed you.
You managed to make her believe

RAY.

Because she loves me.

UNA.

What's wrong with her?
Must be something wrong with her.

RAY.

Don't
Do not say that.
Don't talk about her.
She she has helped me.

UNA.

Do you have any children with her?

RAY.

No.

UNA.

Do you want children?

RAY.

That's not funny.

UNA.

D'you see me laughing?

Actually — it is funny.

(She laughs briefly. He turns away.)

In that photo there's nothing.

Nothing in your face.

Smiling.

You've forgotten.

You've

RAY.

Yes.

Yes I have.

UNA.

Ten years later, eight

eight years

now

you'd be on the registry.

Your name would be there.

Ray would be there.

You'd be

You wouldn't be able to forget.

You couldn't

Peter.

You'd

No one would let you.

It wouldn't just be me.

People would be outside your

surrounding your house.

RAY.

I'm living my life.

A new life that I fought for because I lost

UNA.

Did you ever think about me?

RAY.

I have every right.

I can push it as far away as I

UNA.

What was happening to me?

RAY.

You think I should relive it every day?

This is my life.

You can't.

UNA.

When when that judge

RAY.

You can't come in and

UNA.

Six years.

And when my parents told me.

RAY.

I am entitled to something.

To live.

UNA.

I did the sentence.

I did your sentence.

For fifteen years.

I lost everything.

I lost more than you ever did.

I lost

because I never had

had time to to to *begin*.

We never moved.

That house on that street.

I was talked about, pointed at, stared at.

I lost all my friends.

I

I *kept* my name.

I had to keep my name.

I

Yes.

I relive it every day.

RAY.

If you want me to

whatever it is you want me to

I've taken you seriously.

But if you tell me

You can't think about it every day.

UNA.

I don't have to think.

It's *there*.

RAY.

Is that wise?

No.

To

To let yourself?

To

Does no one tell you it's

D'you not have friends

people who

UNA.

Of course I have friends.

RAY.

Who know that you do this?

UNA.

Yes.

RAY.

And they listen?

They still

UNA.

Yes.

RAY.

What kind of friends are they?

What kind of

UNA.

Don't talk about

RAY.

They *allow* this?

They actually

Are they waiting to hear from you?

How this went?

How

Are they outside?

Did they drive you here?

Are they

UNA.

There's no one with me.

How many times do I have to tell you?

RAY.
Do you
a partner?
A

UNA.
That has nothing to do with this.

RAY.
Does anyone care about you at all?

(Pause.)
I've done the same.
I've brought you in here
Let, let you talk.
And I was
and listened and

UNA.
What about the photos?

RAY.
What do you do?
Do you work?
Are you able to work?
Have you taken time off to

UNA.
The photos.

RAY.
What photos?

UNA.
The photos you took of me.
In your apartment.
Where are they?
They never found them.

RAY.
I

UNA.
The police never found them.

RAY.
They

UNA.
I've seen websites.
Hundreds on websites.

34

Hundreds of nine, ten, eleven, twelve years old.
Younger.
Photographed in
on beds
in bedrooms and
Am I one?
Because these
some of
the photos go back to the seventies
they
you can tell by the room
and people, men *scan* them and put them, they
those kids'll be adults now and not know they're
RAY.
I burnt them.
UNA.
Did you?
RAY.
Yes.
Of course I did.
Of course.
No one ever saw them.
I burnt them before we
Before we left.
And they weren't
You were wearing your clothes, jeans
They
UNA.
Sitting on your sofa.
Lying down.
They have the same photos on those
RAY.
Those sites.
That
Those people.
Those sick bastards.
I was never one of them.
I was never that.
You
you've been told I was, I am, I

They called me that.

They

I spent three years in hell.

More.

UNA.

Yes.

RAY.

What they called me.

Spat on, kicked.

Shit, human shit thrown in my face.

You know I wasn't one of them.

UNA.

How?

RAY.

You know.

UNA.

I don't know you.

I don't know anything about you except that you abused me.

Didn't you?

Didn't you?

RAY.

Yes.

But

UNA.

There's no but.

RAY.

Let me

UNA.

There is no but.

RAY.

Yes.

I did.

But

UNA.

Jesus.

RAY.

I didn't

I didn't

UNA.

Didn't what?

RAY.

    They said in court I, I

    made it sound

    made it look

    that I'd *selected* you.

    I'd chosen

    That day.

    That day of the barbecue.

    At

    When we talked for the first time.

    I didn't come to

    You know.

(On his belt, his cell phone rings.)

    When I spoke to you for the first time.

    I

    Wait.

(He looks at the phone's screen. He turns it off. Pause.)

UNA.

    Was that her?

RAY.

    Yes.

    Can I have some water?

(He takes the bottle of water, drinks from it.)

    I don't know why he invited me, your father.

    I said hello to him on the street when I saw him.

    I helped him with his car once.

    But

    I was surprised when he asked me.

    I wasn't going to come.

    I didn't know anyone there

    Or neighbors who

    But I

    My windows were open and I could smell the barbecue.

    Five doors away.

    The smoke.

    It wasn't to

    because of you

    to

    I'd seen you on the street.

    Around.

But not
Not
UNA.
You were looking at me.
At the barbecue.
RAY.
No.
UNA.
I saw you
RAY.
I wasn't.
UNA.
I felt you
RAY.
I *looked* at you.
I wasn't *looking*.
UNA.
You said why aren't you happy?
You should be happy.
The first thing you said.
RAY.
Yes.
You were sitting on your own.
Not talking to anyone.
You weren't very happy.
That's what I was watching.
You
People tried to talk to you and you you gave them nothing.
You'd
You'd had a fight with your best friend.
Hadn't you?
UNA.
I used to think
After.
If we hadn't fought.
If she'd been there.
It could've been her.
RAY.
How many people were there?
How many guests?

Fifteen, twenty.
In your backyard.
Your parents' backyard and
You know when you are
A person knows
I read this
when they're aroused by children
by under-age
people.

UNA.
You read it?

RAY.
Yes.

UNA.
There's a handbook?

RAY.
There's

UNA.
A checklist?

RAY.
Because when you're aroused by children
when

UNA.
I read some of those books too.

RAY.
So have I.
So did I.
As many as I could find
To to
Yes, a checklist.
It was, yes.
To find out
to
to learn the facts

UNA.
What facts?

RAY.
The facts.
The patterns.
The the cycle.

UNA.
    The cycle?
RAY.
    Of of
UNA.
    Abuse.
RAY.
    Yes.
UNA.
    Can't you say it?
RAY.
    Abuse.
    Abusing.
    There's figures
UNA.
    Were you abused as a child?
RAY.
    No.
UNA.
    You're sure?
RAY.
    Yes.
    For God's sake.
    Don't
    I feel sick.
    I think I'd remember that.
    The lawyer asked me if I *had* been.
    It was better for me if I had been.
    Better better for everyone if I had been.
    I read those books.
    I thought about my life.
    To be sure I wasn't one of them, one of
    Because three years, seven months being told
    asked to ask myself
    interrogate myself.
    Being given no
    Because when you are
    when kids
    when they they do it for
    for a person

but they don't want to to admit
they're shocked
horrified that they
they feel like this.
They stay away.
They're a threat and they know it.
They distance themselves.
They
Because they love them but
they love them too much to
to want to show that love because that love is
They want to protect them.
They stay away from wherever children will be.
But if you're aroused.
Do desire.
And want to want to
feed that desire
they find ways
they
they're always looking for ways to be near them.
To lure them.
These people are
very very careful
are very very deceptive
The greater the deception
the greater the risk
the more they enjoy it.
UNA.
Did you memorize these books?
RAY.
It was a hot day.
The day of the barbecue.
I
and I had a pair of shorts on.
My *only* pair of shorts.
I only ever own one pair at a time.
I wear one pair until they're old and then buy new ones.
Because I don't
UNA.
What

41

RAY.
    Wear shorts.
UNA.
    Are you
RAY.
    I never wear shorts unless it's very hot.
UNA.
    Shorts?
RAY.
    And they were tight shorts.
    It was the style then.
    The
    Don't smile.
    Don't
    I'm trying to tell you.
    Don't
    They laughed in court.
    They laughed at that in court.
    I remember these shorts.
UNA.
    Do you hear yourself?
    Your tight shorts?
    Do you know how
RAY.
    If I had an erection
UNA.
    You're serious?
RAY.
    If I had an erection.
    Aroused.
    I was standing beside you.
    I would've
    I would've walked away from you
    or sat down or
    because when I had an erection in those shorts it was
    You couldn't miss it.
    It was obvious.
    Any person looking could plainly see
    any guest would've seen.
    They would've

And it's not
I know it's not the only
indication
but but it is for me
When I am
when I
turned on I get hard.
I get hard immediately.
But I stayed there.
I stayed there and talked to you.
You were someone's
a neighbor's daughter who
who was annoyed at the world that day.
Not not a
target.
I never
I had a
I was seeing a woman.
And I know they
those people can have relationships
and still do what they do.
But most of them not
don't.
They're loners
Incapable of having a
(Pause.)
UNA.
My parents thought you were
RAY.
What?
UNA.
Shy.
A little dull.
And a loner.
Why didn't you bring your girlfriend.
My dad said you could bring her.
RAY.
She wasn't my girlfriend.
She was

UNA.
    You saw a lot of her.
RAY.
    I only saw her for a few months.
    I can't even remember her name.
    She was dull.
UNA.
    She attacked me once.
    A couple of years later.
    I was with my mother walking on the street.
    She came up to me and slapped my face.
(*Pause.*)
RAY.
    She said you used to glare at her.
    That you were, were after me.
    You'd hang around on the street beside my car.
UNA.
    It's how I made up with my friend.
    I told her about you.
    About talking to you.
    You, you looking at me.
    Flirting.
RAY.
    That was you, not me.
    You
    The notes.
    You wrote notes.
    You put them under the windshield wipers of my car.
    Your girlfriend's ugly.
    She has a glass eye.
    Always one sentence.
    She laughs like a donkey.
UNA.
    That's not
RAY.
    And others.
    Remember the barbecue.
    That was one.
    I had to tell you to stop it.
    Outside the drug store.

44

And you said what was I talking about.
You pretended not to know.

UNA.

I did stop.
I stopped writing them.
I'd have done anything you said.
I wanted you to be my boyfriend.
I wanted to sit beside you in your car and be driven into town.
And for people to see me.
See *us*.
I took a Polaroid of you and
with my friend
we kissed it
we
put it on my pillow and slept beside it.
And I
any excuse.
Brought you cookies and brownies that my mother made.
Asked you to sponsor me for a walk-a-thon.
I
oh I was shameless.
You didn't stop that.
All you had to do was tell my parents.
A stupid girl who had a stupid crush.
But you didn't.
You let it start.

RAY.

You weren't stupid.

UNA.

Yes I was.

RAY.

You weren't.

UNA.

I was too young.
Too too in
love.
Too stupid not to have been older
not to have have
the awareness
the experience.

But that's what you wanted.
I didn't ask difficult questions.
I didn't have any questions *to* ask.
I wanted anything you wanted.

RAY.

No.

UNA.

Yes.
I said yes and I kept saying yes.
Eager to please.
Desperate to please.

RAY.

You don't remember yourself.
What you were like.

UNA.

What was I like?

RAY.

Strong.

UNA.

Strong?
What does that mean?

RAY.

Headstrong.

UNA.

Don't.

RAY.

Determined.

UNA.

Don't.

RAY.

When we started to really talk.
Alone.
When you told me about yourself.
I discovered
You surprised me.
You made me laugh.

UNA.

Laugh?
Did I
what?

Make faces?

RAY.

I

UNA.

Tickle you.

RAY.

You were older than her.

That woman I was seeing.

UNA.

Older?

RAY.

With that stupid laugh.

Yes.

UNA.

How, older?

You're not making any

RAY.

You knew about love.

You knew more about love than she did.

Than *I* did.

You knew what you wanted.

So so impatient.

You couldn't wait to start menstruating.

You told me that.

You were sick of being treated like a child.

The last thing you wanted was to be told you were a child.

UNA.

Jesus.

RAY.

You

UNA.

That's what children *say.*

RAY.

You weren't like other children.

UNA.

I was a girl.

A virgin.

An untouched body.

A

Having it to yourself.

47

Being the first.
Teaching me.
Showing me.

RAY.

No.

UNA.

Coming inside me.
What could I have possibly given you
given you that *wasn't* my twelve-year-old body?
What else could you have wanted?
There was nothing else.

RAY.

There was.
For me there was.

(She walks away from him.)

You were on my mind all the time.
I couldn't get you out.
And I gave in.
I gave in to it.
And it
everything
every day was about how I could see you, talk to you.
I left work early.
I, I'd work on my car on the street.
It didn't need work.
I took things apart, put them back together.
Just to
The engine was perfect.
But I'd
Because you'd be there and we could talk and it was fine.
It was in the open and no one thought anything.
Your parents.
The kids that played there.
But it, it wasn't enough, it
I had to be alone with you.
You remember the
the codes
the signals we had to to meet.
To just speak.
Talk.

To be alone together.

You remember?

I'd call your parents house.

One ring.

UNA.

It meant that she wasn't with you.

You were on your own.

RAY.

And park my car facing right.

UNA.

I forgot that.

And the next day you'd be there to meet me.

In the park.

The public park.

RAY.

It was the only place we could meet.

UNA.

The first time.

In the park.

I'd be so excited.

Knowing you'd be there.

And I ran.

Because you were mine.

You were sitting on a bench reading a newspaper.

And the first thing you said to me

You told me not to sit down beside you.

I had to walk past you.

And I knew why.

RAY.

It was ridiculous.

Stupid place to meet.

I hadn't thought about it.

I, I *didn't* think.

I didn't know what was happening to me.

And you

UNA.

I walked into the bushes.

RAY.

You disappeared.

And started calling out my name.

Ray.

Come here, Ray.

I sat there and

a man

there was a man walking along the path.

You called out again and he looked at me and laughed.

He hadn't seen you.

He didn't *know.*

Only heard your voice.

Ray, come on.

I'm waiting.

And I

I'd been seen but I could still explain it.

Up to that moment I would still be believed.

I could walk away and stop everything.

UNA.

But you didn't.

RAY.

No.

I couldn't.

Whatever was happening

whatever I was thinking

thought about

was in me

made me believe I loved you.

Made me walk across the grass, the

get on my knees and crawl under the branches.

And hold your hand and

and kiss you.

UNA.

And lay down next to each other.

And open my shirt and touch my

my breasts.

And and unzip yourself.

And take out your cock.

RAY.

Not the first time.

UNA.

I'm sorry.

You you *gentleman.*

Not the first time.
The second, the third time.
Both of us lying on a blanket you brought.
A blanket.
I thought it was for me but it was

RAY.
It was.

UNA.
So that twigs and and earth and
wouldn't stick to my clothes.
So no one would suspect.

RAY.
I didn't want us to get caught.

(Pause.)
It never came up in the trial.
The park, the bushes.
The blanket.
I always wondered why.

UNA.
I never told them.

RAY.
Why?

UNA.
I was
I don't know.
You didn't either.

RAY.
No.
They'd have given me ten years.

(Pause.)

UNA.
I was only in court for one day.
Testifying in a separate room.
I never knew what was said.
No one told me anything.
I was at a relative's house.
Not allowed to leave.
No television, no newspapers.
No one told me about the trial.
Even now my mother won't

You remember the name of the town?
Where we
we went.

(Pause.)

RAY.

Yes.

UNA.

There was a beach.
It was dark.
Winter.
All the stores were closed
We walked along the beach.
It was cold.
We held hands.
We could do that because it was dark.
You got a room at a guest house.
I had to stand behind you as you paid the woman.
Keep my head down and run up the stairs.
Did you know her?
That woman.

RAY.

No.

UNA.

I always thought you did.
I don't know why.

RAY.

No.
How would I?
No.
What

UNA.

There were twin beds.

RAY.

Okay.

UNA.

Why not?

RAY.

I've told you why.
It's
I don't want to hear it.

UNA.

I do.

RAY.

We both know what happened.

UNA.

I don't. I don't know everything.

You don't.

You don't know anything.

I want you to know.

What I did for you.

RAY.

What you did for me?

UNA.

Twin beds.

A TV.

Nothing else.

The window looking out at the water.

We undressed.

We had sex on one of the beds.

I don't know how long for.

I saw how much pleasure it gave you.

I liked I could do that.

We did it twice, fucked twice.

You turned me round for the second time.

You made so much noise.

We lay in each others arms afterwards.

I cried a bit.

I don't even know if I came.

Did I come?

(Pause.)

RAY.

I thought you did, yes.

UNA.

What did I do?

How could you tell?

Did I make a noise?

RAY.

You

Your face was flushed

You kept your eyes closed a long time.

(Pause. Una stares at him; recognizing this.)
UNA.

> You said you wanted cigarettes.
>
> You were going to look for a store, a bar.
>
> I wanted to go with you but you said no I had to wait there,
wait for you.
>
> You'd be five minutes.
>
> And you touched me you
>
> kissed me between my legs
>
> your tongue
>
> both of my breasts.
>
> You'd be back in no time.
>
> I lay on the bed.
>
> I listened to your footsteps going downstairs.
>
> I wrapped the sheet around me and went over to the window.
>
> I wanted chocolate
>
> I tried to open it.
>
> Whatever I ate then.
>
> Candy.
>
> Shout to you.
>
> Chocolate.
>
> But the window wouldn't open.
>
> I saw you down below, opening the front gate.
>
> I knocked on the window but you
>
> you were already walking along the street, the middle of the street.
>
> You didn't hear me.
>
> I fell asleep and when I woke up I didn't know the time.
>
> I was sore between my legs but I felt wonderful.
>
> You hadn't come back yet but I was so happy.
>
> My man would be back soon and he would have chocolate for me.
>
> I didn't need to tell him what I wanted.
>
> You knew and you'd bring it to me.
>
> But you still didn't come.
>
> The room was cold.
>
> I got dressed, looked out the window.
>
> Your car was still there across the road.
>
> I could hear talking downstairs, not clearly.
>
> But voices.
>
> I walked down the stairs.
>
> The front door was closed.

The only sound was a TV coming from a room.
The voices were from the TV.
The door was open a bit.
I knocked on the door.
Nothing happened.
No one was there.
I opened the front door and went out.
There was a shout as I was closing the door.
The woman.
I opened
saw her
what are you or
saw her walking towards me
and I, I shut the door and
ran to the gate and out into the street and ran.
I walked into the center of town.
It was late.
Ten on the church clock.
The ferry left at midnight.
There wasn't long.
You were nowhere.
A store was open, lights.
I asked inside if a man had bought some cigarettes.
He told me to get out.
He thought *I* was buying cigarettes.
I tried to describe you but he didn't listen.
Then a bar.
You'd be inside having a drink and a smoke.
But I couldn't go in
I had to
all my courage
wait till two men walked in
follow behind them
and look for you
walking around the bar.
Men making jokes, laughing.
What was I looking for?
You lost, honey?
I said my dad.
The man behind the bar asked me

We said I'd
in trouble
you were my dad.
Told him what you wearing, what you looked like.
He'd seen you.
You'd been in.
Smoked a cigarette, had a drink, then left.
He was concerned, the man.
He asked me my name and I told him.
He wanted to walk with me, help me look.
I said no, no, no, I'm fine, I'm fine.
I kept walking.
Along the main street.
A few people passed me.
I wanted to ask them if they'd seen you but I didn't know what
to say.
I went into another bar.
Everyone's face turning to look at me, shouting, laughing.
I walked on and on.
I walked past houses
getting further from the water.
I walked ten steps, ran ten.
You'd be at the next corner, the next.
Any moment.
And every car was you.
The houses stopped.
I was at the end of the town.
I looked out into the darkness.
I'd gone too far.
I'd walked too far.
I was at the end.
You
I'd missed you.
You were back at the guest house.
Looking for me, wondering where I was.
I'd
I ran.
I ran back.
I thought I was lost and then I wasn't.
I could see the clock above the roofs.

I walked towards it.
It was eleven thirty.
We could still make the ferry.
I ran and ran.
I could see the guest house.
But your car had gone.
I checked
ran up and down looking into all the cars but
and my bag was inside your car
with all my clothes
with everything.
And you were gone.
The clothes I'd brought.
But
and
The room
but it was dark, the window.
I didn't know what to do.
Waited.
I sat on a bench.
I was freezing, hungry.
I wanted to know why you'd gone.
What I had done.
I was crying.
You'd left me.
You'd
Or something terrible had happened.
You'd been killed or drowned or
I couldn't do anything, couldn't go anywhere.
We wouldn't be on the ferry.
We wouldn't be leaving.
I didn't know what to do.
Something had happened.
You wouldn't have left me.
You wouldn't have done that.
I heard midnight.
You weren't coming.
I was alone.
A woman talked to me.
They saw me and crossed the road.

A man and a woman walking their dog.
They asked what I was doing there.
Where did I live?
Who was looking after me?
I went back to their house.
They gave me blankets and called my parents.
I lay on their sofa and listened to her talk to my mother.
The police were there with her.
I felt sick.
I wanted to die.
I was never going to see you again.
I'd have to face all of them
everyone
all of them
alone.
I protected you.
Defended you.
Stayed
stayed true.
I told the police you hadn't touched me.
You'd done nothing.
I was a
I was a runaway.
I wanted to escape my parents, my house, my school.
You'd given me a lift in your car.
You helped me escape.
I'd asked you, begged you.
You'd driven me there and left.
You won't know any of this.
They wanted to do tests.
Take samples out of me.
Doctors, police.
I refused.
No one was going to touch me.
I shouted, screamed
You'd done nothing.
You'd
I wanted you to
I wanted you back.
I

They drugged me.
Held me down and and injected me.
Opened my legs and took
took out your come.
Evidence.
They asked me what you'd done to me.
Then told me what you'd done to me when I wouldn't.
You were only after one thing.
That's why you'd disappeared.
You'd gotten what you wanted.
My my mother screaming at me.
She
The police, the
a woman psychiatrist who spoke
always spoke so quietly.
Adults lie.
They want things from people and they lie to get them and,
and don't
they don't even know they're lying.
They do not know themselves.
I couldn't hear her sometimes.
Had to ask
repeat
repeat what she'd said.
Did I know what I'd done?
Did I know that I'd hurt people?
People who loved me.
Did did I want to hurt them?
And
For days.
What had you said?
What did you promise me?
What words
What words did you use?
And in court I sat in that other room and I spoke.
I cried.
You must have heard me.
I cried more than I spoke.
And then I
I said too much, I

The lawyers were furious with me.
It wasn't what they wanted.
I couldn't help it.
It was you.
You were in the courtroom and I couldn't see you so I shouted.
I had to let you know.
You left me alone.
Bleeding.
You left me
You left me in love.
When they came home at the end
into the house
My parents.
Not home.
The relatives house.
I was in the bedroom, waiting.
They were silent.
They didn't move.
I sat and waited.
They didn't come into the room.
I thought maybe you'd gotten off.
You'd been let go.
You'd be coming back to live beside us.
Until my dad
later
told me six years.
And in the night I woke up and my mother was there.
Leaning over me.
Shouting that *they'd* been tried.
She'd been on the stand.
And my dad had to take her out of the room.
Pull her out of the room.
And
The judge.
What he said about me.
You'll remember.
I had
suspicious
suspiciously adult yearnings.
When my mother told me that I didn't know what she meant.

I hate the life I've had.
You wouldn't know that.
I wanted you to know that.
I knew you'd forget about me.

RAY.
I wrote you a letter.
After a year in there.
I sent one.
They let me send one.
They had to read them first.
Did you get it?

UNA.
No.
I didn't get any letters.

RAY.
They'd have told your parents.

UNA.
What did it say?

RAY.
To forgive me.
Explaining.
Apologizing.
What I'd learned about myself.

(Pause.)
There was another letter
One they wouldn't let me send.
I thought it would be good for you to read it.
I came back.
I was coming back for you.

(Pause.)
I bought

UNA.
Coming back?

RAY.
Yes.
I did buy cigarettes.
I
Listen.

UNA.
Is this what you tell yourself?

RAY.

It's what happened.

I bought the cigarettes but I went

UNA.

Is this what you use?

To to

For this?

To smile in a photo.

RAY.

No.

Listen.

There was a bar.

I

Listen.

I had a drink.

I needed time.

I needed to think, to plan.

The ferry.

How to explain.

What to say.

And I needed a drink.

I needed courage.

It was going to happen.

I walked around for a while.

The streets.

Behind, around.

I knew you were waiting for me.

But I had to

Until I was back there, at the guest house.

Looking up at the window.

The light in the window.

The woman was there.

Stripping the sheets.

She said you'd gone.

You'd run off.

What was going on?

I left her.

I walked out.

You weren't at the car where I thought you'd be.

Or the beach.

I shouted for you.
I thought you were hiding.
I drove into the town looking for you.
I couldn't find you.
I didn't know where you'd go.
Why you'd gone.
I started to panic.
I thought the police would appear any minute, surround my car.
I parked.
I went back into the bar.
The same bar and ordered another drink.
He didn't move, the man there, the same man who'd served me.
He was staring at me.
He asked me about my daughter.
Had, had I found her?
And I
I looked at him and said yes, yes I had, she was fine.
There was another man beside me.
Asking if I *had* a daughter and what was her name.
I
and I
Another man was getting up from his seat.
The first one leaned over the bar, tried to grab me.
I pulled away, swore at them.
They
Told them
Three, four of them after me.
I ran out.
They chased me.
Two kept chasing me.
I hid
ran somewhere, a
I lost them.
I hid there for, I don't know, an hour.
I heard the clock strike midnight.
I got back to the car and, and drove away and
I didn't know if you'd gone to the police or
if I was leaving you
but I couldn't stay.
I drove to where the ferry left from.

If maybe you'd gone somehow, gone there.
Waiting for me there.
I waited till dawn.
Then I knew it was over.
I kept driving.
I didn't know where to go.
I drove west.
I heard the news on the radio.
Safe and well.
Found by a couple walking their dog.
The police were hunting me.
Hunting my car.
They gave out the license plate number.
I kept driving.
Kept to back roads.
I left the car behind.
Walked.
Found a phone booth, called the police.
Waited there till they came.
I'd never have left you there.

(Pause.)

UNA.

But there's no difference.
Leaving or coming back.
There's

RAY.

There is.
For me there is.

UNA.

Better for you.
Easier for you.

RAY.

It's not easier.
It's
The lawyer

UNA.

Why say it?
Why say it now?

RAY.

The lawyer said it sounded better if I had left you there

because it showed I knew the seriousness
the awfulness of what I had done.
That I ran from you.
Never to to return.
Because of what it would sound like to a jury
be *made* to sound like.
That I was going back for
For more.
Because what else would I go back to you for?
When I couldn't find you that night.
I thought something must've happened to you.
I knew you wouldn't leave me.
Someone had taken you.
Someone was
harming you.
Even thought maybe
maybe I should go to the police.
When they found me I was on the floor of the phone booth.
Hugging my knees.
Crying my eyes out.
Because I'd lost you.
I, I hadn't protected you.
It does make me feel better.
That I was coming back.
It does.
Whoever I was then.
It makes me feel better.
UNA.
Why didn't you send the letter?
RAY.
I told you.
They wouldn't let me.
UNA.
There must have been some way.
RAY.
No.
(Pause. She stares at him. The lights shut off suddenly, in the room and in the windows. Ray tries the light switch a few times.)
UNA.
What happened?

65

What happened.

RAY.

I don't.

(Una backs against the wall.)

UNA.

What's going on?

RAY.

I have to go and see.

UNA.

Is something wrong?

RAY.

No.

Wait here.

UNA.

Where are you going?

RAY.

I have to find out what's

Stay here.

Okay?

UNA.

Yes.

RAY.

I'll be one minute.

It's probably a power failure or but

Wait here.

(He opens the door, goes out. Una waits, very still. Outside, distant sound of doors closing. A minute passes.)

UNA.

Ray.

Ray.

(She walks to the door, looks out into the darkness, afraid. She turns back. The light comes back on in the room but not the windows. After some moments, Ray reenters.)

RAY.

They're unbelievable.

UNA.

Who?

RAY.

Them.

All of them.

They left.

UNA.

All of them?

RAY.

Yes.

To go home.

UNA.

Are the doors locked?

Are we

RAY.

No.

No.

I have keys.

I lock up.

UNA.

Why didn't they tell you?

RAY.

I don't know.

They

They're stupid bastards.

What's wrong?

One of them must've just

not thinking.

A stupid joke.

They're

UNA.

You lock up?

RAY.

I have keys.

I'm usually the last

UNA.

You'll lock up tonight?

RAY.

Yes.

Why?

UNA.

Are you the

RAY.

What?

UNA.
>The night watchman?
>The, the
>security.

RAY.
>No.

UNA.
>The janitor?
>Are you

RAY.
>No.

UNA.
>They must think you are to

RAY.
>I'm not.

UNA.
>To leave you here.

RAY.
>I am not

UNA.
>You haven't finished cleaning up.
>You'd

RAY.
>In a

UNA.
>better start.

RAY.
>In a shirt?

UNA.
>Look at all this.

RAY.
>And trousers like these?

UNA.
>You've got

RAY.
>And these shoes?

UNA.
>Some kind of fixation.

RAY.
>It didn't say the *janitorial* staff, the photo.

What d'you mean, fixation?
What?
UNA.
　　Trousers, *shorts*.
RAY.
　　What're you talking about?
　　I'm
　　I have a position here.
(Pause.)
UNA.
　　I don't know who I'm looking at.
RAY.
　　I worked to get this.
　　I worked to get here.
UNA.
　　Do *you* know?
RAY.
　　Everything was finished for me.
　　Closed to me.
UNA.
　　Does *anyone?*
RAY.
　　I slaved.
　　To *not* be a janitor.
　　A drunk.
　　A
　　a waste.
　　To rescue something from the
UNA.
　　You haven't changed.
　　You still just talk
　　talk to get, to
　　Lie and don't even know you're
RAY.
　　Shut up.
UNA.
　　I don't know what to believe, Ray.
　　There's so much to choose from.
　　Do you live in here?

69

RAY.

What?

UNA.

Maybe all

RAY.

What're you talking about?

UNA.

The food is yours.

This is yours.

You live here and you

you never leave.

You never

You don't have anyone.

RAY.

I have someone.

UNA.

You live here and eat here and

RAY.

I found someone.

I

UNA.

Does she know?

Does she know you were coming back to me?

Did you tell her that?

You haven't told her.

Have you?

You haven't told her anything.

RAY.

I wanted to.

I wanted to but

I wouldn't

And we have a life.

I've done better than anything anything I could

UNA.

You

RAY.

Could imagine.

From that phone booth.

From that that

Crying on his knees.

I've
My parents.
Family.
When I was inside.
The friends.
Nothing for me.
Refused to do anything.
My apartment was repossessed.
I had debts.
I had nothing.
But I found her.
And I am the luckiest

UNA.
Jesus.

RAY.
Most most grateful man.

UNA.
Can I meet her?

RAY.
Don't be stupid.

UNA.
But I'm not stupid, Ray.
You said I wasn't stupid.
I want to meet her.
This wonderful woman.
Who'd never forgive you if she knew.
Who'd
Describe her.
What does she look like?

RAY.
Why?

UNA.
C'mon.
What does she look like?

RAY.
No.

UNA.
Is she pretty?
Attractive?

(Ray turns away from her. Una pursues him, getting closer to him.)

Blonde, brunette?

Tall or short?

Smart or stupid?

Ignorant.

You coward.

To live like this.

RAY.

Why don't you shut your mouth?

UNA.

I would hate to be her.

How old is she?

What's the age gap?

How much

RAY.

One year.

She's one year older than me.

UNA.

So she's old like you.

She's sixty.

RAY.

She's not sixty.

UNA.

You're almost sixty.

(Ray turns away from her.)

Is she still sexy?

Does she still turn you on?

RAY.

Yes.

UNA.

What does she do to you?

RAY.

Jesus.

UNA.

What d'you like?

All that sagging skin.

What's she do best?

RAY.

You're ill.

You have

UNA.

I'm not ill.

RAY.

Don't come near me.

UNA.

I'm not ill.

(She picks up a chair, hurls it at him.)

I am not ill.

You are.

(She picks up another. Ray tries to stop her. They struggle together. Una falls to the floor, shouts out in pain.)

RAY.

Are you alright?

UNA.

Get away from me.

(Pause. Una gives a short laugh.)

You have

on your shirt.

It's wet.

Food or

RAY.

Jesus.

UNA.

What is it?

RAY.

I don't know.

It's wet.

Jesus.

have to

(He goes to a locker, opens it.)

Nothing.

I thought there might be another shirt.

(He sits down.)

UNA.

You used to like good clothes.

That jacket you had.

RAY.

I don't know what happened to that.

UNA.

Your clothes now, they're

73

RAY.

I know.

Cheap.

The pay's not great here.

They don't pay me enough for what I do.

I should ask for more.

I like what you're wearing.

(Pause.)

UNA.

Where's the water?

(He picks up the bottle of water, takes it to her. She drinks. Pause.)

I have a job.

I work.

Before, I travelled for a few years.

Now I work.

I make good money.

A few friends.

Not many.

My apartment could be bigger.

I'm a terrible driver.

But my car runs perfectly.

RAY.

How's your mother?

Do you see her?

UNA.

I have no choice.

She sees *me*.

Still still won't trust me.

(She laughs suddenly to herself.)

My mother.

She began to find me boyfriends.

A few years ago.

Eligible men.

Sons of friends, of neighbors.

She invited them over to our house.

We'd drink tea.

It was like the nineteenth century.

Winning my hand.

Because I

I had slept with a lot of men before that.

A lot.
And when I got unhappy.
When I'd had enough
when
when I'd made my parents suffer enough
because I told them
I'd tell them in detail what I did with these men
I stopped.
RAY.
How many?
UNA.
You don't think I'd keep count do you?
RAY.
I don't know.
You might
UNA.
Eighty-three.
RAY.
Do you have someone now?
UNA.
Yes.
We're apart now.
After three years.
But I love him.
I want to love him again.
If we can.
This water.
I need a drink.
A real drink.
My mouth's dry.
RAY.
Beer.
UNA.
Yes.
Is that what you drink?
RAY.
Sometimes yes.
Wine.
Beer would be good.
Do you want to?

UNA.
>   Go for a drink?

RAY.
>   There's a place not far.

UNA.
>   A drink.

RAY.
>   No.

UNA.
>   No.

RAY.
>   My stomach.
>   Too much beer.

UNA.
>   Yeah, I saw that.

(They laugh. Pause.)
>   It's a pigsty in here.

RAY.
>   They're
>   They'll come back tomorrow and eat in here again
>   and not
>   because the janitor
>   the
>   who cleans
>   is the worst.
>   He does nothing.
>   He reads.
>   He has an office and he sits and reads and

UNA.
>   Where is he?

RAY.
>   Gets sick.
>   Always sick.
>   Whenever he feels like it.

(He touches his shirt again.)
>   This is disgusting.
>   It is a pig-sty.

(He runs at the garbage can and kicks it over. It falls, trash spills out. He kicks the trash. Una joins in. They kick together. The trash lies everywhere. They stop, look at each other. They start again. He stops,

out of breath, sits. She goes nearer to him.)
UNA.
     Are you alright?
RAY.
     I think so.
(Pause.)
     I'm going to die at sixty.
     I know I will.
     I've always
     some
     I believe it'll happen.
     Sixty.
     A feeling.
     I've only a few years left.
     A few to go.
     To see you now.
     And you to be unhappy.
     And I am the cause of that.
     I never wanted to hurt you.
UNA.
     You did.
(They are near to each other. He puts his hand out, strokes her.)
RAY.
     I did think about you.
     I *do* think about you.
UNA.
     What do you think?
     Do you think about me then?
RAY.
     Yes.
     Yes, I do.
     It's all I have.
UNA.
     In that room?
RAY.
     Yes.
     Touching you.
     Holding you.
UNA.
     Fucking me?

RAY.
    Yes.
    Fucking you.
UNA.
    Do you masturbate?
    Do you come?
RAY.
    Yes.
(They stare at each other. They kiss. It gets more intense. They begin to undress each other. They lie down. Ray pulls away.)
    No.
    I can't.
    I can't.
UNA.
    I want you to.
RAY.
    No.
UNA.
    Why not?
RAY.
    I'm sorry.
    I can't.
UNA.
    Am I too old?
(Outside the room, from some distance away, an adult female voice calls out.)
VOICE.
    Peter?
RAY.
    It's alright.
(He seems not to have heard it.)
UNA.
    Did
VOICE.
    Peter?
(He stares at the door.)
UNA.
    Is it her?
RAY.
    Yes.

(The voice calls, fainter, further away than before.)
VOICE.

Peter, are you here?
RAY.

She's at the other end of the building.

We can
UNA.

What?
RAY.

We have to get out.
(Pause. The sound of the door handle turning. Una moves over to the far wall. Ray walks towards the lockers. The door opens and a girl of twelve enters.)
GIRL.

You're here.

Peter.

You're here.
RAY.

Hello.
(The girl goes to him, puts her arms around him.)

What're you doing?
GIRL.

We're looking for you.

Where have you been?
RAY.

I was here.
(He moves away from her.)

I'm busy.

I'm changing.
GIRL.

What are you doing?
RAY.

Look at the mess in here.
GIRL.

I'll help you.
(She bends down to pick up the trash.)

You eat too much.
(She laughs to herself)
RAY.

No.

Don't darling.

Don't.

(Firmer.)

Drop it.

(The girl drops the trash, stares at him.)

Go and find your Mom.

Tell her I'm coming.

Tell her I'll see both of you at the entrance.

I'll get the car and I'll meet you at the entrance.

Wait there for me.

I'll be a few minutes.

Go.

GIRL.

Come with me.

RAY.

I can't.

GIRL.

Why?

RAY.

I can't yet.

I will.

Five minutes.

I have to lock all the doors.

GIRL.

Why can't I stay here with you?

RAY.

You shouldn't even be here.

You shouldn't be in here.

It's not allowed.

You have to go now.

(The girl sees Una.)

GIRL.

Who's she?

Peter?

Why is she there?

Why is she hiding?

RAY.

She's not hiding.

UNA.

I'm not hiding.

(The girl moves closer to Ray.)
GIRL.
> Peter, who is she?

RAY.
> A friend.

GIRL.
> Does she work here?

RAY.
> No.

UNA.
> We were just talking.

RAY.
> And you've interrupted us.

GIRL.
> Are you coming with us?

UNA.
> No.

RAY.
> Darling

GIRL.
> Do you know my mom?

UNA.
> No, I don't.

GIRL.
> What's her name?

RAY.
> Una.

UNA.
> You should go now.

RAY.
> You should.

GIRL.
> I want to stay with you.

RAY.
> Darling you can't.
> You have to find Mom.

UNA.
> Go.
> Please.
> Go.

You have to.
(Una guides the girl out of the door. Silence.)
She's not yours?
RAY.
No.
Another man.
You're not my my
I don't have to tell you everything.
(Una groans.)
Don't.
Don't.
What you're thinking.
UNA.
You can't.
Oh God.
RAY.
No.
I could never.
Believe me.
(He moves closer to her.)
I take care of her.
I look after her.
I would never.
(He takes hold of her, getting more insistent.)
I would never do that.
I would never.
Believe me.
You have to believe me.
(He stops.)
Never.
*(He embraces her, stroking her face. He kisses her. She doesn't respond.
He breaks apart from her.)*
I've never
loved
never desired anyone that age again.
Ever.
UNA.
Just me.
RAY.
Yes.

Just you.
You were the only one.
(They stare at each other. Pause. Both of them look at the door. Ray takes a step towards it.)
I have to go to them.
UNA.
No.
RAY.
They need me.
(She goes to him, holds him.)
UNA.
No.
RAY.
Let me.
Let me go.
Let me.
UNA.
You can't.
RAY.
I have to.
(She's clinging tighter. He breaks from her. She wants to hold onto him. Ray exits.)
UNA.
Ray.

End of Play

PROPERTY LIST

Cell phone
Bag with tissues, water bottle, piece of paper
Trash

SOUND EFFECTS

Cell phone ring
Doors

NEW PLAYS

★ **GUARDIANS by Peter Morris.** In this unflinching look at war, a disgraced American soldier discloses the truth about Abu Ghraib prison, and a clever English journalist reveals how he faked a similar story for the London tabloids. "Compelling, sympathetic and powerful." *–NY Times.* "Sends you into a state of moral turbulence." *–Sunday Times (UK).* "Nothing short of remarkable." *–Village Voice.* [1M, 1W] ISBN: 978-0-8222-2177-7

★ **BLUE DOOR by Tanya Barfield.** Three generations of men (all played by one actor), from slavery through Black Power, challenge Lewis, a tenured professor of mathematics, to embark on a journey combining past and present. "A teasing flare for words." *–Village Voice.* "Unfailingly thought-provoking." *–LA Times.* "The play moves with the speed and logic of a dream." *–Seattle Weekly.* [2M] ISBN: 978-0-8222-2209-5

★ **THE INTELLIGENT DESIGN OF JENNY CHOW by Rolin Jones.** This irreverent "techno-comedy" chronicles one brilliant woman's quest to determine her heritage and face her fears with the help of her astounding creation called Jenny Chow. "Boldly imagined." *–NY Times.* "Fantastical and funny." *–Variety.* "Harvests many laughs and finally a few tears." *–LA Times.* [3M, 3W] ISBN: 978-0-8222-2071-8

★ **SOUVENIR by Stephen Temperley.** Florence Foster Jenkins, a wealthy society eccentric, suffers under the delusion that she is a great coloratura soprano—when in fact the opposite is true. "Hilarious and deeply touching. Incredibly moving and breathtaking." *–NY Daily News.* "A sweet love letter of a play." *–NY Times.* "Wildly funny. Completely charming." *–Star-Ledger.* [1M, 1W] ISBN: 978-0-8222-2157-9

★ **ICE GLEN by Joan Ackermann.** In this touching period comedy, a beautiful poetess dwells in idyllic obscurity on a Berkshire estate with a band of unlikely cohorts. "A beautifully written story of nature and change." *–Talkin' Broadway.* "A lovely play which will leave you with a lot to think about." *–CurtainUp.* "Funny, moving and witty." *–Metroland (Boston).* [4M, 3W] ISBN: 978-0-8222-2175-3

★ **THE LAST DAYS OF JUDAS ISCARIOT by Stephen Adly Guirgis.** Set in a time-bending, darkly comic world between heaven and hell, this play reexamines the plight and fate of the New Testament's most infamous sinner. "An unforced eloquence that finds the poetry in lowdown street talk." *–NY Times.* "A real jaw-dropper." *–Variety.* "An extraordinary play." *–Guardian (UK).* [10M, 5W] ISBN: 978-0-8222-2082-4

DRAMATISTS PLAY SERVICE, INC.
440 Park Avenue South, New York, NY 10016 212-683-8960 Fax 212-213-1539
postmaster@dramatists.com   www.dramatists.com

NEW PLAYS

★ **THE GREAT AMERICAN TRAILER PARK MUSICAL music and lyrics by David Nehls, book by Betsy Kelso.** Pippi, a stripper on the run, has just moved into Armadillo Acres, wreaking havoc among the tenants of Florida's most exclusive trailer park. "Adultery, strippers, murderous ex-boyfriends, Costco and the Ice Capades. Undeniable fun." –*NY Post.* "Joyful and unashamedly vulgar." –*The New Yorker.* "Sparkles with treasure." –*New York Sun.* [2M, 5W] ISBN: 978-0-8222-2137-1

★ **MATCH by Stephen Belber.** When a young Seattle couple meet a prominent New York choreographer, they are led on a fraught journey that will change their lives forever. "Uproariously funny, deeply moving, enthralling theatre." –*NY Daily News.* "Prolific laughs and ear-to-ear smiles." –*NY Magazine.* [2M, 1W] ISBN: 978-0-8222-2020-6

★ **MR. MARMALADE by Noah Haidle.** Four-year-old Lucy's imaginary friend, Mr. Marmalade, doesn't have much time for her—not to mention he has a cocaine addiction and a penchant for pornography. "Alternately hilarious and heartbreaking." –*The New Yorker.* "A mature and accomplished play." –*LA Times.* "Scathingly observant comedy." –*Miami Herald.* [4M, 2W] ISBN: 978-0-8222-2142-5

★ **MOONLIGHT AND MAGNOLIAS by Ron Hutchinson.** Three men cloister themselves as they work tirelessly to reshape a screenplay that's just not working—*Gone with the Wind.* "Consumers of vintage Hollywood insider stories will eat up Hutchinson's diverting conjecture." –*Variety.* "A lot of fun." –*NY Post.* "A Hollywood dream-factory farce." –*Chicago Sun-Times.* [3M, 1W] ISBN: 978-0-8222-2084-8

★ **THE LEARNED LADIES OF PARK AVENUE by David Grimm, translated and freely adapted from Molière's Les Femmes Savantes.** Dicky wants to marry Betty, but her mother's plan is for Betty to wed a most pompous man. "A brave, brainy and barmy revision." –*Hartford Courant.* "A rare but welcome bird in contemporary theatre." –*New Haven Register.* "Roll over Cole Porter." –*Boston Globe.* [5M, 5W] ISBN: 978-0-8222-2135-7

★ **REGRETS ONLY by Paul Rudnick.** A sparkling comedy of Manhattan manners that explores the latest topics in marriage, friendships and squandered riches. "One of the funniest quip-meisters on the planet." –*NY Times.* "Precious moments of hilarity. Devastatingly accurate political and social satire." –*BackStage.* "Great fun." –*CurtainUp.* [3M, 3W] ISBN: 978-0-8222-2223-1

DRAMATISTS PLAY SERVICE, INC.
440 Park Avenue South, New York, NY 10016 212-683-8960 Fax 212-213-1539
postmaster@dramatists.com www.dramatists.com

NEW PLAYS

★ **AFTER ASHLEY by Gina Gionfriddo.** A teenager is unwillingly thrust into the national spotlight when a family tragedy becomes talk-show fodder. "A work that virtually any audience would find accessible." *–NY Times.* "Deft characterization and caustic humor." *–NY Sun.* "A smart satirical drama." *–Variety.* [4M, 2W] ISBN: 978-0-8222-2099-2

★ **THE RUBY SUNRISE by Rinne Groff.** Twenty-five years after Ruby struggles to realize her dream of inventing the first television, her daughter faces similar battles of faith as she works to get Ruby's story told on network TV. "Measured and intelligent, optimistic yet clear-eyed." *–NY Magazine.* "Maintains an exciting sense of ingenuity." *–Village Voice.* "Sinuous theatrical flair." *–Broadway.com.* [3M, 4W] ISBN: 978-0-8222-2140-1

★ **MY NAME IS RACHEL CORRIE taken from the writings of Rachel Corrie, edited by Alan Rickman and Katharine Viner.** This solo piece tells the story of Rachel Corrie who was killed in Gaza by an Israeli bulldozer set to demolish a Palestinian home. "Heartbreaking urgency. An invigoratingly detailed portrait of a passionate idealist." *–NY Times.* "Deeply authentically human." *–USA Today.* "A stunning dramatization." *–CurtainUp.* [1W] ISBN: 978-0-8222-2222-4

★ **ALMOST, MAINE by John Cariani.** This charming midwinter night's dream of a play turns romantic clichés on their ear as it chronicles the painfully hilarious amorous adventures (and misadventures) of residents of a remote northern town that doesn't quite exist. "A whimsical approach to the joys and perils of romance." *–NY Times.* "Sweet, poignant and witty." *–NY Daily News.* "Aims for the heart by way of the funny bone." *–Star-Ledger.* [2M, 2W] ISBN: 978-0-8222-2156-2

★ **Mitch Albom's TUESDAYS WITH MORRIE by Jeffrey Hatcher and Mitch Albom, based on the book by Mitch Albom.** The true story of Brandeis University professor Morrie Schwartz and his relationship with his student Mitch Albom. "A touching, life-affirming, deeply emotional drama." *–NY Daily News.* "You'll laugh. You'll cry." *–Variety.* "Moving and powerful." *–NY Post.* [2M] ISBN: 978-0-8222-2188-3

★ **DOG SEES GOD: CONFESSIONS OF A TEENAGE BLOCKHEAD by Bert V. Royal.** An abused pianist and a pyromaniac ex-girlfriend contribute to the teen-angst of America's most hapless kid. "A welcome antidote to the notion that the *Peanuts* gang provides merely American cuteness." *–NY Times.* "Hysterically funny." *–NY Post.* "The *Peanuts* kids have finally come out of their shells." *–Time Out.* [4M, 4W] ISBN: 978-0-8222-2152-4

DRAMATISTS PLAY SERVICE, INC.
440 Park Avenue South, New York, NY 10016 212-683-8960 Fax 212-213-1539
postmaster@dramatists.com   www.dramatists.com

NEW PLAYS

★ **RABBIT HOLE by David Lindsay-Abaire.** Winner of the 2007 Pulitzer Prize. Becca and Howie Corbett have everything a couple could want until a life-shattering accident turns their world upside down. "An intensely emotional examination of grief, laced with wit." *—Variety.* "A transcendent and deeply affecting new play." *—Entertainment Weekly.* "Painstakingly beautiful." *—BackStage.* [2M, 3W] ISBN: 978-0-8222-2154-8

★ **DOUBT, A Parable by John Patrick Shanley.** Winner of the 2005 Pulitzer Prize and Tony Award. Sister Aloysius, a Bronx school principal, takes matters into her own hands when she suspects the young Father Flynn of improper relations with one of the male students. "All the elements come invigoratingly together like clockwork." *—Variety.* "Passionate, exquisite, important, engrossing." *—NY Newsday.* [1M, 3W] ISBN: 978-0-8222-2219-4

★ **THE PILLOWMAN by Martin McDonagh.** In an unnamed totalitarian state, an author of horrific children's stories discovers that someone has been making his stories come true. "A blindingly bright black comedy." *—NY Times.* "McDonagh's least forgiving, bravest play." *—Variety.* "Thoroughly startling and genuinely intimidating." *—Chicago Tribune.* [4M, 5 bit parts (2M, 1W, 1 boy, 1 girl)] ISBN: 978-0-8222-2100-5

★ **GREY GARDENS book by Doug Wright, music by Scott Frankel, lyrics by Michael Korie.** The hilarious and heartbreaking story of Big Edie and Little Edie Bouvier Beale, the eccentric aunt and cousin of Jacqueline Kennedy Onassis, once bright names on the social register who became East Hampton's most notorious recluses. "An experience no passionate theatergoer should miss." *—NY Times.* "A unique and unmissable musical." *—Rolling Stone.* [4M, 3W, 2 girls] ISBN: 978-0-8222-2181-4

★ **THE LITTLE DOG LAUGHED by Douglas Carter Beane.** Mitchell Green could make it big as the hot new leading man in Hollywood if Diane, his agent, could just keep him in the closet. "Devastatingly funny." *—NY Times.* "An out-and-out delight." *—NY Daily News.* "Full of wit and wisdom." *—NY Post.* [2M, 2W] ISBN: 978-0-8222-2226-2

★ **SHINING CITY by Conor McPherson.** A guilt-ridden man reaches out to a therapist after seeing the ghost of his recently deceased wife. "Haunting, inspired and glorious." *—NY Times.* "Simply breathtaking and astonishing." *—Time Out.* "A thoughtful, artful, absorbing new drama." *—Star-Ledger.* [3M, 1W] ISBN: 978-0-8222-2187-6

DRAMATISTS PLAY SERVICE, INC.
440 Park Avenue South, New York, NY 10016 212-683-8960 Fax 212-213-1539
postmaster@dramatists.com www.dramatists.com